Contents

Words appearing in the text in bold, **like this**, are explained in the Glossary.

 Find out more about what it's like to have cancer at www.heinemannexplore.co.uk

What is cancer?

Cancer is a serious illness that can last for several months or years. You cannot usually see cancer, and you cannot catch cancer from somebody else.

Cancer can affect people of all ages.

What's it Like?

Cancer

Angela Royston

young Explorer

Heinemann
LIBRARY

www.heinemann.co.uk/library
Visit our website to find out more information about **Heinemann Library** books.

To order:
☎ Phone 44 (0) 1865 888066
▤ Send a fax to 44 (0) 1865 314091
▢ Visit the Heinemann Bookshop at www.heinemann.co.uk/library to browse our catalogue and order online.

First published in Great Britain by Heinemann Library, Halley Court, Jordan Hill, Oxford OX2 8EJ, part of Harcourt Education.
Heinemann is a registered trademark of Harcourt Education Ltd.

Editorial: Sarah Shannon and Richard Woodham
Design: Ron Kamen, Victoria Bevan and Celia Jones
Picture Research: Maria Joannou and Kay Altwegg
Production: Amanda Meaden

Originated by Dot Gradations Ltd
Printed and bound in China by South China Printing Company

10 digit ISBN 0 431 11225 8 (hardback)
13 digit ISBN 978 0 431 11225 1 (hardback)
09 08 07 06 05
10 9 8 7 6 5 4 3 2 1

10 digit ISBN 0 431 11231 2 (paperback)
13 digit ISBN 978 0 431 11231 2 (paperback)
10 09 08 07 06
10 9 8 7 6 5 4 3 2 1

British Library Cataloguing in Publication Data
Royston, Angela
  Cancer – (What's it like?)
  362.1'96994

A full catalogue record for this book is available from the British Library.

Acknowledgements
The publishers would like to thank the following for permission to reproduce photographs:
Alamy pp.**7**, **8**, **26**; Alamy p.**19** (SW Productions); Corbis pp.**25**, **28**, **29**; Harcourt Education pp.**4**, **9**, **13**, **15**, **17**; Photodisc p.**27** (Getty Images); Science Photo Library pp.**14**, **24**; Science Photo Library p.**10** (Andrew Syred); Science Photo Library p.**11** (CNRI); Science Photo Library pp.**20**, **22** (Colin Cuthbert); Science Photo Library p.**21** (Doug Martin); Science Photo Library p.**5** (James Stevenson); Science Photo Library p.**12** (John Greim); Science Photo Library p.**16** (Mauro Fermariello); Science Photo Library p.**23** (Paul Avis); Science Photo Library p.**6** (VVG); Science Photo Library p.**18** (Will & Deni McIntyre).

Cover photograph of a young boy reproduced with permission of Getty Images.

Every effort has been made to contact copyright holders of any material reproduced in this book. Any omissions will be rectified in subsequent printings if notice is given to the publishers.

The paper used to print this book comes from sustainable resources.

Cancer affects the **cells** in a part of the body. It may affect the **blood**, the **lungs**, the **stomach**, or another part of the body.

Skin cancer is one of the few cancers that you can see.

What are cells?

Your body is made up of millions of tiny **cells**. Your skin is made of skin cells and your **blood** is made of blood cells.

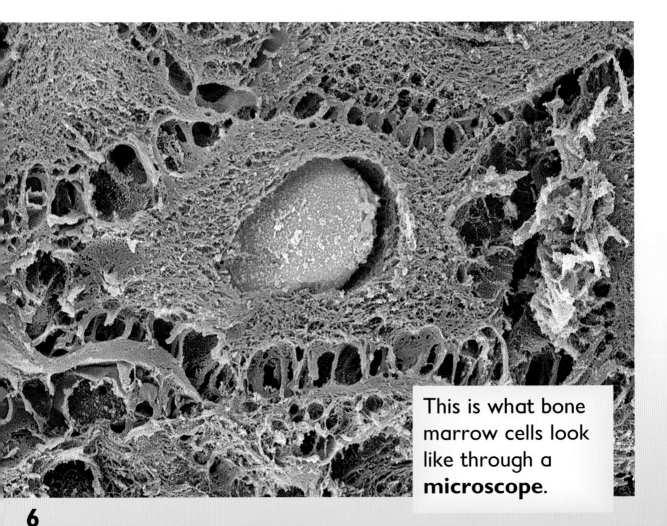

This is what bone marrow cells look like through a **microscope**.

This boy's body will make new skin cells to heal the graze.

Your body is making new cells all the time. The new cells replace old and damaged cells. A person has cancer when cells in a part of the body begin to grow out of control.

Who gets cancer?

People of all ages can get cancer. Older people are more likely to get cancer than younger people. No one knows for sure what causes some cancers.

Cancer can affect people of all ages.

Some types of cancer are caused by the way people live. Smoking causes many types of cancer. An unhealthy **diet** can also make a person more likely to get some types of cancer.

Smoking can cause a type of cancer called lung cancer.

Types of cancer

Cancer usually affects one part of the body. Leukaemia is a type of cancer that affects some of the **cells** in the **blood**.

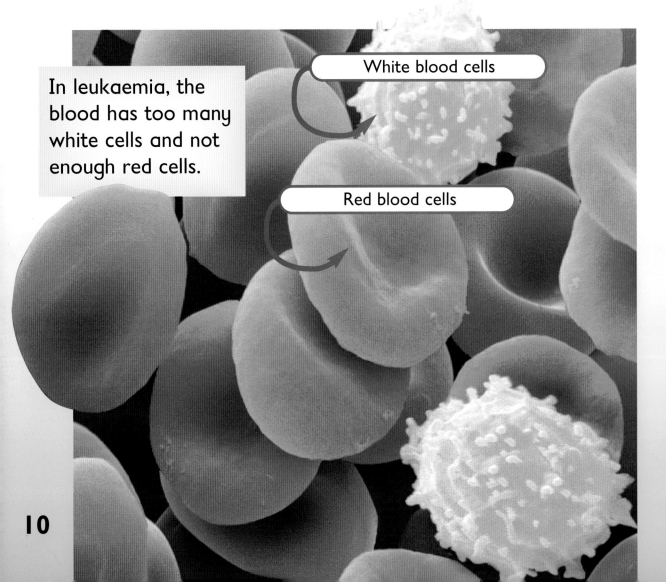

In leukaemia, the blood has too many white cells and not enough red cells.

White blood cells

Red blood cells

In this picture you can see a tumour growing in the bone of a finger.

Other kinds of cancers can cause **tumours**. These are lumps of cancer cells. Tumours can grow in many parts of the body.

How is cancer detected?

Hospitals can test for different types of cancer. Sometimes the **cells** in a small amount of **blood** are tested. Cells from a lump or **tumour** can also be tested.

A simple blood test can detect some types of cancer.

A specially trained person looks at the cells through a **microscope** to see if they are harmful cancer cells.

Cells can be seen clearly using a microscope like this one.

Scans

Most **tumours** can be found by using a machine that can take pictures of the inside of your body. The picture is called a scan.

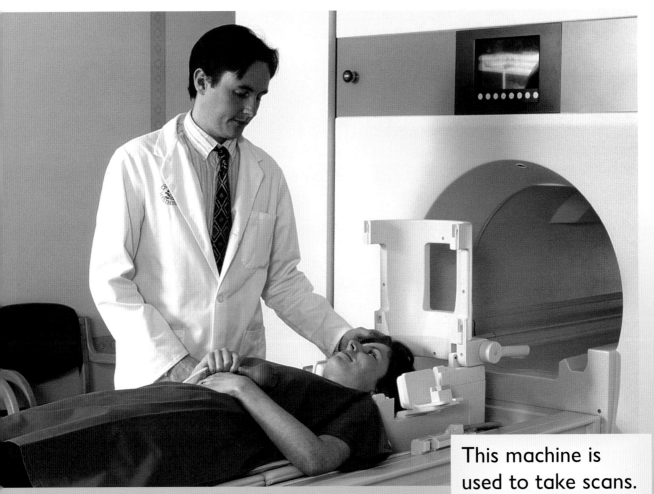

This machine is used to take scans.

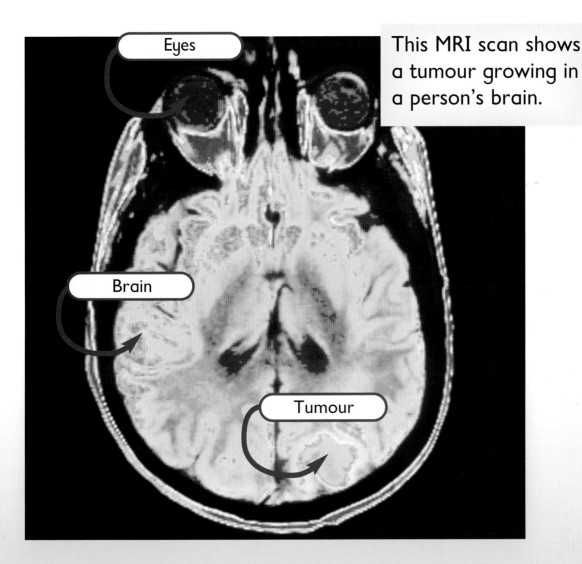

Eyes

Brain

Tumour

This MRI scan shows a tumour growing in a person's brain.

An **MRI scan** can look at the whole body. A doctor then looks at the pictures the machine takes to see if there is a tumour.

How is cancer treated?

Cancer can be treated in different ways. A **surgeon** may cut away the **tumour** during an **operation**.

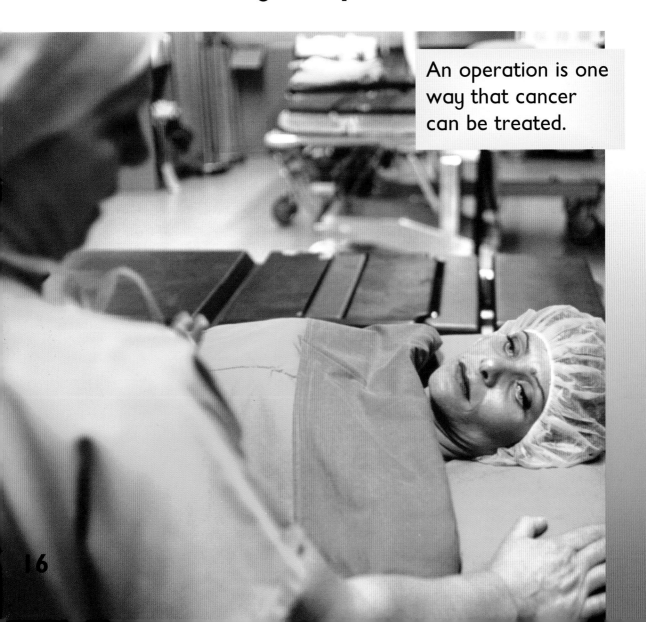

An operation is one way that cancer can be treated.

Before an operation to remove a tumour, the person is given an **anaesthetic**. This makes them sleep very deeply. They feel nothing and wake up when the operation is over.

This boy is recovering after a long operation.

Radiotherapy

Sometimes the cancer **cells** can be killed without the person having an **operation**. In **radiotherapy**, cancer cells are usually killed using **X-rays**.

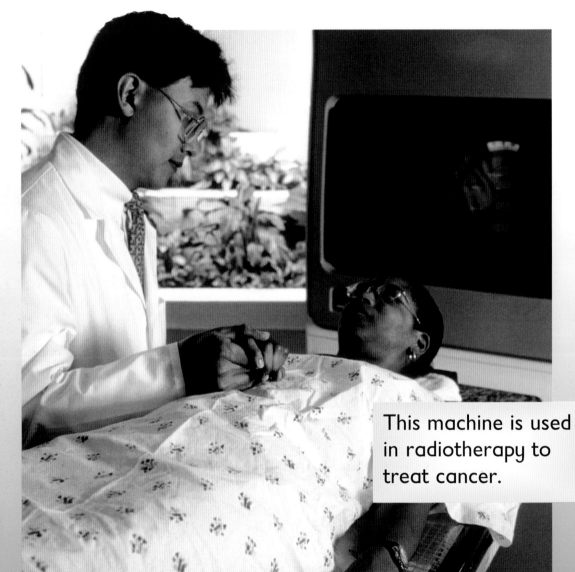

This machine is used in radiotherapy to treat cancer.

Radiotherapy does not hurt and it takes only a few minutes. Many people have radiotherapy five days a week for eight weeks.

This girl is writing the dates of her treatments on a calendar.

Chemotherapy

In **chemotherapy**, the person is given **drugs** that are carried around the body by the **blood**. The drugs try to stop the cancer **cells** growing.

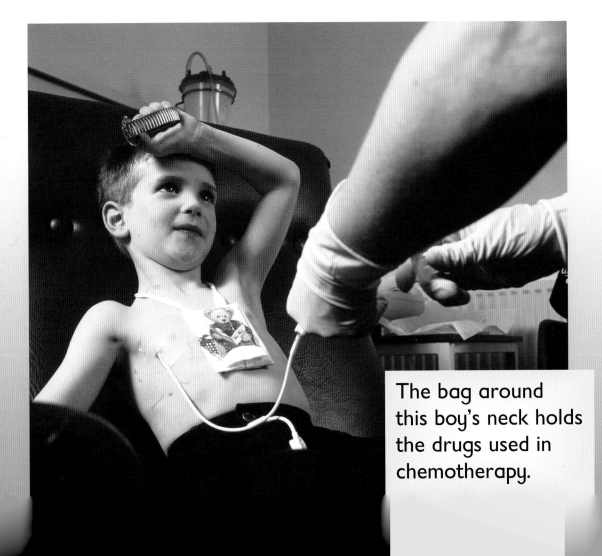

The bag around this boy's neck holds the drugs used in chemotherapy.

Chemotherapy uses a mixture of different drugs.

Sometimes doctors use chemotherapy to try to stop cancer coming back. Leukaemia is one type of cancer that is treated by chemotherapy.

After treatment

The **drugs** used to kill cancer **cells** are very powerful. They can affect other parts of the body, but just for a short time.

The drugs used to treat cancer have made this boy lose his hair.

The hair soon starts to grow back after treatment finishes.

The **treatment** for cancer can make some people feel very sick. Feeling sick and losing hair are called side effects. The person soon feels well again, though, and their hair grows back.

Getting better

When the **treatment** chosen for a person is over, all the cancer **cells** in their body should have gone. The person is then said to be in **remission**.

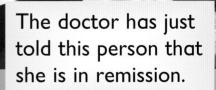

The doctor has just told this person that she is in remission.

Sometimes the cancer comes back and the person has to be treated again. Sometimes the treatment does not work and, sadly, the person dies.

The sooner a cancer is found, the more likely the treatment will work.

25

Life as usual

When the **treatment** has finished the person can begin to carry on with their normal life again. It may take a few months for a person's hair to grow back completely after **chemotherapy**.

Most people who have had cancer can play sports and do everything that other people do. However, it can take a long time for life to get back to normal after treatment has finished.

Preventing cancer

People can do things to make it less likely that they will get some types of cancer. Using sun cream helps to protect you from skin cancer.

Using sun cream helps to avoid sunburn, which can cause cancer.

Not smoking and not drinking too much alcohol can help to avoid many cancers. Eating healthy food helps to avoid other cancers.

Eating healthy foods like those pictured here can help avoid many cancers.

Find out more

CancerBACUP

CancerBACUP offers cancer patients, their friends, and their families information, advice, and support to help people affected by the disease.

www.cancerbacup.org.uk

CLIC (Cancer and Leukaemia in Childhood)

This charity has been set up to help children with cancer or leukaemia and their families.

www.clic.uk.com

Cancer Research UK

Cancer Research is an organisation that aims to find a cure for cancer. The CancerHelp website includes stories written by people who have had the disease.

www.cancerhelp.org.uk

 Find out more about what it's like to have cancer at www.heinemannexplore.co.uk

Disclaimer

All the internet addresses (URLs) given in this book were valid at the time of going to press. However, due to the dynamic nature of the Internet, some addresses may have changed, or sites may have ceased to exist since publication. While the author and publishers regret any inconvenience this may cause readers, no responsibility for any such changes can be accepted by either the author or the publishers.

Glossary

anaesthetic something that stops you feeling pain

blood red liquid pumped around the body by the heart

cell one of the smallest parts of all living things

chemotherapy way of treating diseases such as cancer using drugs

diet the food and drink usually eaten by a person

drug something used to treat disease

hospital place where sick or injured people are treated

lung part of the body used for breathing

microscope instrument that makes very tiny things look big enough to see

MRI scan picture taken of the inside of the body

operation treatment involving opening up part of a person's body in order to repair something that is wrong

radiotherapy way of treating cancer using X-rays

remission when a person no longer has cancer cells in their body

stomach part of the body where food you swallow goes first of all

surgeon person who performs operations

treatment way of trying to cure an illness

tumour lump that grows in the body

X-rays beams that can pass through the soft parts of the body but not through bones

---

More books to read

Barr, Cranston, Leblanc, and Restivo, *You and Your Cancer: a Child's Guide* (B.C. Decker Inc, 2001)

Donovan, Sandra, *Amazing Athletes: Lance Armstrong* (LernerSports, 2004)

Index